F✳CK

THAT GUY

and **ANYONE** that stands in the way of **YOUR GREATNESS**

Shennoah Miller

For permission requests, write to the author, at:
Shennoah Miller
P.O. Box 26 Tire Hill, Pa. 15959
1HBIC.SMiller@gmail.com

F*ck That Guy And ANYONE Who Stands in the Way of Your GREATNESS/ Shennoah Miller. —1st ed.

Paperback ISBN: 979-8-9853372-0-4
Hardcover ISBN: 979-8-9853372-1-1

Dedication

This book is dedicated to my son Riley.
My love for you gave me the strength I needed to keep going on days
I wanted give up. Being the mom you deserved and a woman you could
be proud of gave me the motivation I needed to turn my pain into power
and the inspiration to create a better version of my life for me and for
you. I could not be more proud of the young man you are becoming and
I'm confident momma raised you right and you'll never be "That Guy" to
anyone. I love you more than anything, even peanut butter.

All my love,

Mumsy

Yo B*tch!

Yo B*tch! That's right, I'm talking to you! You're the one that picked up a book titled *F*ck that Guy*, so don't act shocked or hurt when the first line you see is "Yo B*tch!" It has become a salutation that is very near and dear to me. It was how my homegirls lovingly referred to me when they called to check in during the throes of my divorce. "Yo B*tch, how you doing? Yo B*tch, you okay? Yo B*tch, you need us?" No matter what, my peeps were there with a "Yo B*tch" and all the support I needed, and now I'm going to do the same for you! Whatever headspace or emotional state you're in, that's where we'll start this journey together.

If you've picked up this book, it means you are ready to take action and make the changes you need to reach your maximum potential. You are ready to take ownership and control of your life. You are ready to tell all the haters to f*ck off. You are done letting "that guy" (or anyone) put you down and you are ready to get in the driver's seat. All of the words that used to hurt you and keep you down will now be used to fuel and motivate you. It is time to unapologetically accept and embrace who you are. You must find a way to dig deep down in the trenches of your soul and TURN YOUR PAIN INTO POWER! Together we are going to build your self-esteem and confidence to unprecedented levels. You won't ever walk into a room feeling self-conscious again. Gone are the days of self-doubt and bashfulness. You'll walk into every room with your shoulders back and head lifted knowing you're the baddest b*tch around. Your confidence is going to intimidate some folks, but that's their problem, not yours.

I used to feel bad that I intimidated people and I really couldn't understand why they were intimidated by me. It finally clicked that it was the confidence I possessed, and they lacked, that was intimidating. I didn't have to stop being confident and self-assured to make insecure people feel better. That's crazy talk! I want to align myself with other confident, self-motivated, strong people. Insecure assholes will put you down and try to make you feel bad about being confident. And do you know why they do that? Because they are insecure. They need to make other people feel bad about themselves so they can somehow feel better about themselves. These are not the kind of people you need in your circle. You need people who are strong and successful, people who motivate you to be the best version of yourself. You need people who appreciate and respect your confidence.

We've all had those types of friends, boyfriends, husbands, family members who constantly have something negative or passive aggressive to say about us to try to make themselves look better. We've all gotten that backhanded compliment, right? Something like this sound familiar? "Your hair looks great, but you were much prettier as a blonde." Guess what Karol...I didn't ask you what color you prefer my hair because I don't f*cking care if you like it or not. Maybe it was something more serious that destroyed your self-esteem. You may have suffered through an emotionally and mentally abusive relationship with someone who always said you weren't good enough. Being constantly ridiculed or belittled will keep you in a perpetual state of turmoil, unhappiness, confusion, and low self-esteem, but "Yo B*tch" we're here to tune out that negative bullsh*t and let our greatness shine through. I hope this book can help you get out of a toxic situation and be the best version of yourself. It's time to say "F*CK THAT GUY" and focus on rebuilding yourself. Together we're going to build the foundation of a strong, confident you that owns and loves who she is! Let's get to work!

Let's Be Clear

Before we dive in and get too far, let me be clear. This is not a book about hating men. Don't let the book title fool you. I'm not here to bash men or tell you they're all pieces of sh*t. I'm not a member of any she-woman, man-haters group. The title is an ode to a favorite saying my bestie and I would say every time my ex pulled another stunt or had some vile things to say. I would call her crying with woes of what he had done and for a long time she listened and empathized, but after many of these phone calls her common response became "F*ck that Guy," which always made me laugh and dried the tears for a bit.

This is a book about taking back your power from whoever stole it. This is a book about self-reflection, self-evaluation, and evolution. This is a book about rising above the bullsh*t and overcoming adversity. It's about finding strength you never thought possible. It is about learning how to accept and love yourself. This book is about owning who you are and being comfortable in your skin. The intent of this book is to let you know you're not alone. That other people have been where you are. I've been where you are. My goal is to help you through this time in your life by sharing my experiences and stories. My hope is that by sharing my journey from pain to power that you will find your way to the other side like I did. Maybe some of the things that helped me will help you through. Everyone's journey is different, but I hope this book can serve as a source of inspiration and motivation for you. I hope that some of the things that helped me through the darkest time of my life may help you too. This book is aimed at helping you realize your greatness and making the best out of your life. I want to see you grow, thrive, and succeed. So, in summary, I do not hate men. What I hate are people that bring negativity, pain, and anxiety into the lives of others and hold them back from being the best versions of themselves. In my case, it just happened to be "that guy."

Damage Control

Before you can make any changes you first have to assess your situation and do some self-reflecting. You're going to have to ask yourself some hard questions and you're going to have to be brutally honest if you want to make real and lasting changes.

Who was it who said you couldn't do it or you weren't good enough? Who made you feel less than the amazing chick you are? An ex-boyfriend/husband perhaps? An asshole at work or a phony friend? No matter who it was, they can go f*ck themselves! You don't need that sh*t and you don't deserve it. Maybe you think you won't be able to get through this breakup or divorce or you'll never get over him, but I'm here to tell you, you can and you will. You will get over it and your life will be better than you could have ever imagined. You will soon realize THAT GUY was holding you back. You weren't living up to all your greatness because he was snuffing it out. I'm here to tell you there's no guy you can't live without. My ex told me nonstop that no one liked me, not even my family, and I believed him. When you are told something repetitively, over time you accept it as the truth. I believed people didn't like me because I was too intense, too confident, too this, too that. Whatever the negative feedback of the day was, that's what I thought was true. I didn't dare show an ounce of confidence or pride because then I was accused of "thinking I was better than everybody." It didn't matter what I did because no one was going to like me.

Well, the truth is, it turns out I was married to one of the insecure assholes I told you about earlier. He wanted me to believe all of these terrible things about myself because it made him feel better about himself. My increasing success only fueled his insecurities, so he had to try to keep me down and make me feel bad about myself. Of course, I didn't realize at the time that this was happening. If I had been aware that I was being mentally and emotionally abused, I may have taken action and left a lot sooner. But that's what abusers do. They make you think you are the problem. It has taken years of self-reflection to see that he was the problem, not me. When I got rid of him, everything changed. The proverbial chains were broken and the sky was the limit for me! You can get rid of whatever jerk is holding you down and holding you back. You can break your pattern of abusive or unhealthy relationships for good. It's time to stop being codependent and become I.N.D.E.P.E.N.D.E.N.T. just like Beyoncé told us to. You are going to love your new sense of self-worth and seeing how capable you are without him in your life. You got this!

This book is going to give you a roadmap to getting your life back on track. I will share stories and personal experiences that hopefully motivate, inspire, or teach you something along the way. I will help you identify "That Guy" in your life who is holding you back or holding you down. I will help you figure out why you are allowing yourself to accept that kind of treatment from anybody. We will go through this journey of self-discovery, self-acceptance, and self-love together until you realize the greatness inside of you and take the action necessary to stop being a victim and start taking control. By the end of this book you will be on the road to being the best version of yourself. The exercises in this book will force you to get real with yourself and create an actionable plan for your success. The ultimate goal is to create a self-awareness that will allow you to achieve personal growth and reach your full potential. Oh my dear, you are going to reach a level of badassery you didn't know you had in you. You are going to leave THAT GUY'S head spinning and wishing he never did you wrong. Don't be afraid to fall, be prepared to fly.

"But what if I fall, oh my dear, but what if you fly."

ERIN HANSON

Stop all the Clichés Already

I know people are trying to help, but when you are in the eye of the storm, all the clichés in the world won't help ease your pain. The truth is, your friends and family have good intentions. They want to see you through this, they just don't know what to do for you so they say things like, "you're better off without him," "you'll get through this," "God wouldn't give you more than you can handle," "you'll find someone else." You catch my drift. It used to absolutely infuriate me when people said these things to me. How did they know what I could handle? How could they be so sure I was better off without him or that I'd get through this? It sure didn't seem like I was going to get through it. I felt like I was spinning out of control. I was convinced my life was over and I was positive I could not live without him. They had to be wrong. They couldn't understand the pain and anguish I was going through. They couldn't feel the physical pain of the heartbreak. I wished they'd just stop saying all of those things and let me wallow in my misery.

If you're like me, I'm sure you've heard all of these clichés and more from your well intentioned friends and family. These people love you and don't want to see you in pain and agony. They are only trying to help, and the fact of the matter is all of these clichéd sayings are probably true, even if you don't believe any of them right now. I'm sure you're not convinced that "you'll get through this" or "you'll be better off" when it feels like your life has been destroyed. When you can't eat or can't stop eating, can't sleep at night, cry uncontrollably, and cannot find joy in anything you do, you are not going to be convinced so easily that "everything happens for a reason." Don't deflect the anger you are feeling toward the people who are trying to help you. Just know that the people who love you may not have the words to make you feel better, but they are trying to help you rally and pull through this dark time. Some of them may have been through a similar situation and can empathize with what you're going through, but if they haven't been mistreated, neglected, or hurt by someone the way you have, they may not be able to completely grasp the scope of your pain.

The end of any relationship can be painful and overwhelming. Even though it may be for the best, your life is going to change. You are about to head down an unknown path and that is scary. If you are going through a breakup or a divorce, it can be a death of sorts. It symbolizes the end of not only a relationship but also the life you thought you were going to have. When someone passes away our lives go on, but they are different than they were before. Divorce can feel the same way. The marriage or relationship has died, but your life will go on. I want you to use this as an opportunity for a new beginning. You need to mourn your loss and accept that you are moving in a different direction now. You have to process your grief before you can move on and find positive healthy relationships.

Time to pause for some self reflection. What is the unhealthy relationship in your life that is coming to an end? When someone says you will be better off, do you believe it? Are you ready to get "that guy" out of your life? I want you to write down what you are feeling. Acknowledge your feelings. Own them. Accept them. You can't move forward until you come to a place of healing and growth.

_____

_____

_____

_____

_____

_____

_____

_____

_____

_____

_____

_____

_____

_____

_____

_____

Change Your Perspective

Life has a way of taking us where we're supposed to be, which isn't always where we want to be. I get it. You had a different vision for your life. You had it all planned out. Your personal life, relationship, marriage, kids, career, you knew exactly what you wanted in all of these areas. You could picture it all, but surprise, life had an alternate vision for you. You didn't sign up for this or consent to a change of plans, but good ol' life flipped the script and the direction your life was going, and you now have to alter your vision and change your route to get to a new destination. If you're a control freak like me, accepting a plan you didn't come up with is not something you do very well. I fought it so hard. I used so much of my time and energy trying to regain control and create the circumstances I wanted. There could be no deviation from my plan. I wouldn't allow it. The harder I fought, the more exhausted I became. I couldn't relinquish control or accept that my life was taking a different direction. This wasn't what I planned for.

I married this man and we were going to have a life together and that was that. I had invested so much of my time, 15 years, I couldn't just let it all be thrown away. I had to fix it. I could repair the situation if I willed it hard enough. I couldn't just say goodbye to the last 15 years of my life and the rest of my future without any return on the investment of my time. That wasn't right. It wasn't fair that I committed to this relationship and had no choice in whether it was over or not. I just could not reconcile that loss of time with nothing in return.

We followed his path and his career while the things I wanted took a back seat. I was living in a place I hadn't chosen with my life and career goals on hold because I loved him and I loved our family. When you're married, you're a team, a unit and it makes sense to compromise and make sacrifices, but when my marriage ended, I couldn't come to terms with the loss of my time. I put his needs before mine and look at what I got in return. It felt like a slap in the face. Actually, it felt more like a closed fist punch and a kick to the gut, not some silly little slap. I lost all of this time, and to make matters even worse, I had to START OVER and I had no idea how to do that. I didn't know who I was or what I wanted without him. That is scary as f*ck, but you have to mourn the end of the relationship and who you were when you were in it to find the new version of yourself.

The loss of time came up again and again with friends that had ended long term relationships or marriages. Like me, they could not let go of the loss of that person or the time they had given to him/her. It feels like you just have to forget all the memories, the good times and the bad are lost forever, but what I realized and what I told my friends is that similarly to when we lose a loved one to death, we don't have to forget all of the good times we had with them. Even though your relationship is over, it doesn't mean the time and experiences never meant anything. That time is part of your journey and part of your story. That part of the story is over and it is human to feel anger or sadness or grief that this part of your story has ended. Give yourself permission to feel the grief and pain. Yeah, yeah "you'll be better off without him," but before you can be better off without him, you have to accept that he is gone and the life you thought you were going to have is gone. Don't punish yourself for having feelings of loss and sorrow. Allow yourself to process this grief and loss in whatever way is most cathartic for you. If you don't allow yourself to grieve, you will carry the anger, bitterness, and sadness with you and never be able to fully heal and reach your full potential. Let go of what you thought you were supposed to be and you will find out who you were supposed to be. Rediscover yourself. I'm not going to tell you that "you're going to get through this." You're a smart cookie. You'll realize you got through this when you get there.

Self Reflection Exercise

How much time did you invest in your relationship

How does it make you feel now that this chapter has ended?

How can you overcome the negative feelings and replace them with positive ones?

What are some of your favorite memories?

What did you learn during this time in your life?

How did you evolve and change during the course of the relationship?

What positive experiences can you take away?

What can you improve on so you don't continue to make the same mistakes?

Here's something that helped me. If I could blame my ex for all the bad things that happened, shouldn't I thank him for all of the positive things as well? I had to find a different perspective and a way to channel the anger and let it go. I had to find a positive spin on this situation or I was going to self-destruct. Side note—I came pretty close to self-destructing several times on this journey (but we can venture down that fun little road in another chapter). I decided to compose a thank you letter of sorts to my ex to help me see the lessons I had learned and what I had gained along the way. I never thought I'd write a thank you letter to my ex, but here goes nothing...

A Thank You Letter to My Ex

I hated him so much. Hate may not even be a strong enough emotion to describe the resentment I felt toward him, and rightfully so in my opinion. I wished him nothing but ill will. I wanted him to feel all of the pain and hurt that I did, multiplied by 10. He deserved everything and anything that came his way. He stole everything from me. I'm not just talking about physical possession or monetary assets (although he did a good job of getting his greedy mitts on all of those things). What he took from me was much more valuable than money. He took my sense of security and my ability to trust. He wasted my time and created a life based on lies. He blindsided me around every corner and hurt me in every way he could think of. He had an innate ability to kick me just as I was about to get back on my feet. He did despicable and deplorable things to me. His cruelty and lack of compassion were bar none. All of the hateful, cruel words were unwarranted and unnecessary. I thought my life was over, that I couldn't possibly survive or go on without him. I blamed him for all of my pain and suffering, and truly hated him with every part of my being for destroying our family and our marriage. Part of the hatred was being scared that I couldn't do it on my own. The fear of the unknown. Although we didn't have a healthy, happy marriage, I knew what to expect and became accustomed to it. Without that dysfunction, who would I be and what would my life be like? Starting over scared the bejesus outta me, but I didn't have a choice, now did I?

I'm not sure when exactly, but at some point, all of the pain and suffering started to dissipate. I took one day at a time and the fears simmered away on their own. I could do this. I was doing it. I had to do it. My life was moving forward and I was shocked at all of the good things that were happening, things that would have never happened if I was with him. Slowly but surely, I was coming to the realization that he was the negative force holding me back from reaching my full potential. My life wasn't over because he was gone. It was just about to begin and take a whole new direction that I could have never dreamed of. What I thought was the worst thing to ever happen to me turned out to be the best thing that could have happened to me. So instead of harboring all the anger and resentment, I started harnessing that energy to put into other endeavors. As it turned out, I was able to accomplish things I never realized, and that's when I began to understand I shouldn't hate him, I should thank him. And so I composed a letter of thanks to show him my gratitude.

To the man who vowed to "take me down,"

I want to say thank you. Thank you for setting me free from the emotional and mental abuse that I endured for years. I would have convinced myself to keep trying to fix "us" forever, but your actions set me free. I would have never realized that I didn't have the power to fix you. Thank you for underestimating me because that motivated me to try harder and fueled my desire to succeed. Thank you for putting me through hell. Because of you, I can appreciate all of the blessings in my life much more. Thank you for freeing all of the negative energy and headspace you took up so that I could focus on positivity and creativity. Without you controlling my thoughts and emotions, my mind was free to think of new ideas and business ventures. Thank you for making room in my life for more fulfilling and meaningful relationships. Because of you, I have some of the best friendships and relationships I have ever had in my life. The friendships that were present while we were together became even stronger once you were out of the picture. People I would have never allowed into my life have become part of my inner circle. Because of your cruelty, I was shown immense kindness and compassion everywhere I turned. Thank you for taking your negative energy and attitude out of my world and allowing the good vibes to flow in. Thank you for no longer impeding my ability to be authentically me. Without you diminishing my self-esteem and self-worth, I can thrive and grow. I no longer believe the lies you tried to sell me. Thank you for showing me that I can be pushed to the brink and come back stronger than ever. Thank you for teaching me that I thrive in times of adversity and that I have the ability to rise above and grow from difficult situations. Thank you for proving that I am strong enough to stand on my own two feet and that I am better off without you. Thank you for choosing the path you did so that I could take the path to become the best version of myself.

Writing this letter showed me that I could turn this negative experience into a chance to learn and grow. I surprised myself by recognizing that there could be hope found in the most difficult situations. Obviously I never gave him this letter (although maybe he'll buy a copy of this book and get to read it), but that wasn't the point. This exercise was therapeutic and healing for me. It may seem odd to write your ex a thank you letter, but I recommend you give it a try. It will help you see the situation in a whole different light. If you can blame him for all of the bad things that happened, you should give him proper thanks for all of the good things that have come your way now that he's gone.

Letter to Your Ex

You Don't Have to Forgive Him

Gasp. That's right. I said it. You don't have to forgive him. Before you jump to the conclusion that I am an evil, bitter, unforgiving b*tch, hear me out. Forgiving someone may be what you need to get closure and healing in order to move forward. I completely understand that and I'm not suggesting that forgiveness is a negative thing in any way. In my opinion, forgiving a person is not the only way to move forward. You can rise above and let go of anger and resentment, and that doesn't always mean offering your forgiveness. That has to be a personal choice, and for me, I didn't feel that that's what I needed to do in order to let go of the past and get on with my life. I got so sick and tired of people telling me I needed to forgive my ex so I could move on. That forgiving him was about me not him. It sounded like a bunch of bullsh*t to me. If I didn't want to forgive him I didn't believe that it had to be part of my healing process. I am quite capable of moving on and moving forward without giving him the forgiveness he doesn't deserve. Forgiveness is earned. Why would I forgive someone who isn't sorry? My ex hasn't shown any remorse or regret. He didn't ask for my forgiveness or try to reconcile any of the things he did to me. He doesn't lie awake at night thinking "gee I hope Shennoah forgives me." So no, I don't feel like I need to give him the GIFT of forgiveness that he doesn't deserve, but don't get it twisted. Just because I don't forgive him doesn't mean I will waste any more energy or headspace thinking about him. It doesn't mean that I will stay caught up in the past or expect an apology. It means that I have come to a point of acceptance and self-growth where I can move my life forward in a positive direction, and he doesn't factor into that at all.

For a long time, I wanted an apology. I thought he owed it to me, and he probably did. All the things he did to me and said about me, I felt any decent human would feel the urge to apologize to someone for those kinds of things. Especially when said someone is the mother of his child and the person he spent 15 years with. I expected him to realize the error of his ways and come to me and say he was sorry. And then I realized I was absolutely insane to think that would ever happen. This man has not shown an ounce of sympathy or remorse for what he has done. Why on earth would he apologize when he was trying so hard to make everyone believe he was the victim. If he apologized, that would mean all of the bullsh*t he told everyone to make himself look like a victim was a lie. He certainly couldn't let down that façade. This is the man who had vowed to take me down. When they handed out moral compasses, they skipped right over him. Clearly waiting for an apology from this man would be a futile waste of time, and I may have mentioned ad nauseam that I DO NOT have time to waste. I needed to get on with the life that was out there waiting for me. I needed to reclaim my power and my identity and do things that fed my soul. And so, I did. Slowly the longing for an apology and for him to validate the hurt he caused me was replaced by empowerment. I started meeting new people and trying new things. I never missed the opportunity for a new experience or adventure. I focused on all the awesome opportunities in front of me and didn't look back at the cloud of smoke left behind. I focused my energy on new friendships, strengthening relationships, and self-growth. I became motivated to work on myself and realized that had nothing to do with him. My life moved on. Yes, it changed. It's not what I planned or expected. It was better than I could have ever imagined. That didn't come from forgiving him. It came from a conscious decision coupled with hard work and a desire to succeed. It had nothing to do with him and everything to do with me. I'm not trying to give forgiveness a bad rap. I think it can be healthy and healing to forgive people. If forgiveness is a means for you to move on or feel better, then by all means forgive away, but I am telling you the act of forgiveness is not the only way you will be able to move on. Instead, choose not to give the negative people or negative thoughts space in your mind. Free up the place in your mind and in your heart that is holding grudges for people and give that space to experiences that deserve that time and space in your life. The act of forgiving is the only way some people can open up their hearts and let the positive forces back in. All I'm saying is you don't have to subscribe to the notion that you owe someone forgiveness. You don't have to forgive someone who isn't sorry. It is a choice and a gift to forgive someone who has done you wrong and caused you harm. It is also a choice to let them or the things they've done to you define you. So don't let that guy define you. If he is decent enough and offers an olive branch or an apology and you want to forgive and forget, good on you. If he's an asshole and you don't choose to forgive him, that's cool too. But don't wait for an apology you may or may never get to move on and don't feel like you have to give obligatory forgiveness to move your life in a positive direction. Don't give anyone that type of power or control. It's time to say, "F*ck that guy I'm moving on."

Revenge is the Best Medicine... I Call Bullsh*t on That

Revenge is the best medicine. It's so cliché (remember how I hate clichés) and so untrue. Revenge is not the best medicine at all. It won't heal your wounds or make you feel better. Getting revenge isn't going to magically make you forget what your ex did to you. You may think seeing someone else suffer will make you feel better, but I assure you it won't. You know what is good medicine that will make you feel better? Not giving a sh*t about what is going on in your ex's life. When you get to the point on your journey when you don't care what your ex is doing or what happens to him, then you can begin healing. When I ran out of f*cks to give about what was going on with my ex, I could spend my time giving more f*cks about the things I cared about. Not giving a f*ck meant that I wouldn't spend the time or energy it took to give so much of a thought about him.

Believe me. I spent my fair share of time wishing, hoping, and praying for sweet revenge, so I totally get it if you are dying to see the universe stick it to that guy! I wished my ex all the ill will the universe could muster up and send his direction. That Guy deserved the worst of the worst, and I spent a lot of time trying to think of ways to help the universe impose doom and gloom on his life. I ran through different scenarios in my head (and out loud) that would give me the revenge I desired. I employed my girlfriends to listen to these creative tactics time and time again in hopes they would agree with me and somehow put my evil plots into motion.

I hoped his new relationship would fail miserably and he would feel the pain and agony of heartbreak that I felt. I wanted him to feel the financial strain I was experiencing. Let's just say I wasn't sending him well wishes. I wanted him to lose his job so he would feel the financial strain and pressure that he put me through, but that didn't happen either. I spent so much time and energy wishing and waiting for the universe to produce any of these scenarios so I could experience that sweet, sweet revenge that would be the medicine I longed for so badly. If these plots played out the way I saw them in my head, I would be vindicated and validated, but as fate would have it, the universe did not bestow any of these negative forces on my ex. Quite the opposite of everything I wished for was actually happening. The new relationship continued to flourish and grow. They bought a house, got engaged, had a baby, and got married. He did not get fired from his job or shunned by the community. His life was moving forward while I stayed stuck and focused on revenge. The revenge I was after so badly was not the cure for my hurt and pain. The best medicine I could give myself was to quit spending my valuable time and energy seeking revenge, because it wasn't going to change anything. Spending so much time seeking revenge was the opposite of good medicine or as Jon Bon Jovi would say "Bad Medicine." Continuing to seek revenge will only serve to prolong your hurt and despair. The pursuit of justice and validation is a frivolous one that is only going to keep you focused on that guy instead of focused on you and your healing. You have to quit focusing your energy on getting back at him because what you're really doing is continuing to focus your energy on him and he doesn't deserve it. F*ck that guy, remember?

When you redirect the energy you are expending trying to get back at him onto yourself and your growth, your life will start to take a more positive direction. The best medicine is allowing yourself to break out of that negative vortex you are trapped in so that you can begin to heal. If you want medicine that is good for your soul, revenge is not what you are looking for. Spending time with people that love you and add value to your life, that is good medicine. Focusing on new activities or experiences you enjoy is good medicine. Going back to school, pursuing a new business venture, or taking your career to the next level is good medicine. Going on adventures, booking a vacation, enjoying a spa day with friends is good medicine. Find your passion. Find your why. Find what sets your soul on fire and spend your time on those things, not on revenge and not on that guy!

Girl, Keep Your Cool

Listen, I'm not here to judge anyone. I lost my sh*t on more than one occasion when I was going through my divorce, so I'm not here to be a hypocrite and tell you not to lose yours. I know keeping your emotions in check can be nearly impossible when you are experiencing so many different feelings at once. Why do emotions overpower logic and make us act in ways that aren't typical of our normal behavior? Wouldn't it be amazing if we could think clearly and make rational decisions during difficult, emotionally charged circumstances? I don't know about you, but that doesn't come naturally to me when I am put in stressful situations. I like to think I'm intelligent and logical in most circumstances, but there's no denying I'm a passionate person. I love hard and I fight hard. I wear my emotions on my sleeve and one glance at my face will reveal what I'm thinking. That fire and passion smothered the logic right out of me and caused me to act "crazy," and that's exactly what he wanted. He knew exactly how to push my buttons to get the reaction he wanted out of me. He controlled me all those years and I was still a puppet reacting to his words and actions just like he wanted me to. His passive-aggressive tactics got under my skin and worked every single time. The way I was acting painted me in a very negative light and fit the narrative he created about me. I knew what he was doing, but I fell into the trap every time. The deeper into the trenches I went, the more erratic and emotional I became. I was not going down a very good path. Things were about to get more out of control than I ever could have expected. The thing about your breaking point is you don't know what it is until you get there, and once you get there it's too late. I was pushed to the brink, and I met my breaking point and reached one of the lowest points in my life. It wasn't a good look, but it was a wake-up call.

A Little Diddy

This little diddy isn't about Jack and Diane, this one's about Shennoah and Ran. I am sharing this story of one of the worst days of my life with you as a cautionary tale of how quickly things can spiral out of control if you do not seek the help that you need. I'm going to give you the abbreviated version for two reasons: 1. To protect my son and his feelings and 2. Because the details are a bit fuzzy because of the state of mind I was in when the incident occurred.

I was in a very fragile state mentally and emotionally. I was losing everything, my marriage, family, house, money, and hope. I really had nothing else to lose accept one thing that mattered the most to me, my son and then it happened. My son was with his father for the evening as scheduled, but I just had a gut feeling that something was off. I just had that mother's intuition that something was wrong. I could not get a straight answer from anyone about where my son was. Yes, he was with his father, but not where they were supposed to be. Here's where I'll gloss over some of the details and skip ahead to the part where I lose my sh*t. It took some searching, but I came to find out that his father and girlfriend had moved in to a new place and taken my son there without telling me. This conflicted with the terms of our custody agreement and turned me into a raging momma bear trying to protect her cub, however, my actions only hurt my baby bear and served to make me look like a lunatic.

I found myself in there driveway screaming and crying and causing such a ruckus that the police were called. The next thing I knew I was being handcuffed and thrown in the back of a police car and

hauled to the police barracks. There it was, ROCK BOTTOM. I offi-
cially had nothing left to live for. In that moment, I probably would
have preferred to die. They had taken it all, even my baby boy.

There I sat in the police station a broken shell of a human. They
took my fingerprints and my mug shot while I cried uncontrollably.
I made one phone to my best friend in the middle of the night and
she showed up to get me. She drove me home in silence. There was
nothing left to say. She told me to get help. Urged me to talk to a
counselor and get medicated, but she didn't say I told you so. She
just dropped me off and headed home.

I am sharing my story with you in hopes that you never have a story like this one. As bad as it was, it could have been worse. I could
have faced criminal charges, spent time in jail, lost my job, or lost
custody of my son. Don't let your situation spin out of control like
I did. Find ways to manage your stress and emotions. Get counseling, talk to your doctor, join or start a F*ck that Guy community
group. Do whatever it takes so that you don't have a little diddy
like this one.

I found some ways to help channel the emotions: running, yoga,
and spinning were my go-to stress relievers. I immediately set an
appointment with a doctor and a counselor. I began regular ses-
sions with my counselor and started taking prescribed medication.
Slowly I began to return to the land of the living. I wish I had done
all of these things before I lost my sh*t, but I didn't. Can't look
back in that damn rearview mirror and change it, but I could look
forward and face the road ahead much better now that I had the
guidance and tools to get me there.

So, if anyone gets how hard it can be to keep it together, it's me!
Keeping your cool can be nearly impossible, especially when someone is purposefully and often tactfully trying to get a rise out of

you. You want to fight back. You can't let him get away with saying those things about you or doing those things to you. You want to make him pay. You can't let him get away with this sh*t. While I'm not here to judge you, I am here to tell you that every time you react to his negative bullsh*t, he is getting exactly what he wants. As long as you react, he remains in control. You are giving him the power to be your puppet master. This will only serve to cast a negative light on you while he sits back and tells everyone how crazy you are and how your actions are proving his point. You have to find ways to block out the bullsh*t and redirect your emotions. Don't let him push your buttons!! Don't find yourself in the back of a cop car like I did.

Don't Let Your Emotions Overpower Your Intelligence!

I told you some of my stress relievers: yoga and running are my go tos. Maybe you like a bubble bath or cuddling up with a good book. Everyone is different. It doesn't matter what it is, just find what works for you and make it a habit!

Take a moment and jot down some activities that help you destress and calm down.

_____   _____

_____   _____

_____   _____

_____   _____

_____   _____

_____   _____

What other resources are available to you? Find the resources in your area. Do it. Do it now. Get the information and write it down and then call and make your appointments. You're worth it!

Doctor:
_____

Counselor:
_____

Support Group:
_____

Therapy:
_____

Crisis Hotline:
_____

Online groups:
_____

Don't be Afraid to be Scared

I know it sounds like an oxymoron, but before you say "girl, what are you talking about?" let me explain what I mean. Don't be afraid to feel your feelings, whatever they may be. It is okay to be scared or afraid, sad, mad, angry, or any other emotion on the spectrum. It is your right to feel however you want to feel and you don't have to be afraid to be honest and real about that. There's no doubt you are feeling unsure of what the future holds. You are probably questioning every decision you make and wondering if it is the right one. You may feel scared in one moment and angry in the next. Some days may seem impossible to get through while others are smooth sailing. A breakup or divorce is an emotional and painful event. You don't have to pretend you are happy every day. If someone asks how you are, you don't have to give the socially acceptable answer of "I'm fine, how are you?" if that isn't how you really are. Saying you're fine doesn't make it true, and it prevents the people who care about you from being there for you and giving you what you need. The more open and honest you are about how you are feeling and what you are going through, the more likely you are to heal faster. You know why? Because when you are honest with yourself and with others, they can help you overcome the things you are dealing with.

I had a very dear friend who was going through a very similar experience that I had three years earlier. She called me one afternoon from work and said, "What did you do when you wanted to cry at work?" My response, "I cried at work." I know some people may think this is horrible advice. That you've got to hold it together when you're at work or in public. I'm not suggesting you just go to work everyday and be a blubbering basket case, but the truth of the matter is, where we are physically doesn't dictate or control how we are feeling. You may be at work, soccer practice, yoga class, or wherever when a sad memory hits you or you're feeling overwhelmed or scared about your situation. Wherever you may be, it is still okay to feel however you are feeling. People are more understanding and compassionate than you think.

I found the more that I opened up and shared my story and my experiences with the people around me, the more people rallied around me in support and shared their stories. The more people I had in my corner the less scared I became. The unknown is daunting simply because it is unknown. I was afraid I couldn't make it on my own. My whole life was about to change and that was scary as f*ck. I didn't need to feel embarrassed that I was scared. Who wouldn't be afraid to start their whole life over? I didn't need to feel ashamed that I was crying at work. I was broken-hearted and hurting. You may be feeling that way too and I'm here to tell you don't be afraid to show your emotions. Don't be scared to look weak or admit you need help. That's exactly what I told my friend in that moment. She shouldn't be feeling shame and embarrassment that her relationship has ended. That is a completely human and normal way to feel.

Your emotions may change by the day or the hour or the minute. You may feel like you are on top of the world one minute with your sh*t pulled together, and the next you may fall apart. You will never heal and move on if you don't allow yourself to feel what you're feeling and deal with those feelings accordingly. The reality of your new life is scary, but it is also exciting. Don't hide from it. Embrace the fear. Feel it. Push through it and overcome the fear so that you get to experience what is on the other side. Admitting you're scared is half the battle. It takes courage to admit our shortcomings and challenges, but when we conquer them, oh what a sweet feeling.

My sweet friend was so afraid of the life she knew was coming to an end that she couldn't see she had been given the opportunity to start over. She had a clean slate. She could do, be, go wherever she wanted to. Her life wasn't over. She was in a position to break free from THAT GUY and start over wherever and however she wanted. Scary, yes. But also liberating and exciting.

I can relate to her fear all too well. I used to be afraid of everything. NO joke. Literally afraid of everything and anything. I let it consume me. I didn't admit I was scared. I would just make excuses to not do or try things. And you know where that got me? Nowhere. Being afraid to say I was scared caused me to miss opportunities and let life pass me by. Now when something scares me, I acknowledge it. I say that I'm afraid and ask myself, what's the worst thing that could happen? But I wasn't going to let that happen to the new me. I wasn't going to be consumed by fear of the unknown. My aha moment was bound to happen. It had to. This chapter was going to be much different than the one before it.

My light bulb moment happened on a trip to Niagara Falls with a new beau. I was having a great time, but deep down I was scared by many of the new things we were doing. I have always been deathly afraid of heights. This fear is not conducive to riding an open air tram across Niagara Falls from one side to the other. It is very high up and runs very slowly across the gorge. It looked amazing, but I didn't know if I could bring myself to get on. I also didn't want to embarass myself or make my potential love interest think I wasn't up for a good time or adventure so I said sure, let's do it. We bought tickets and I stood in line nervously, not knowing if I would get on or not. Then the cable car pulled in and it was time to go. I had to make a choice. Face my fear and get my ass on that car, or wait and watch from the sidelines. I got my ass on there, and to this day, it is one of my favorite experiences. I got to experience the most epic view with an amazing guy that I would have missed out on if I let fear hold me back. I would have regretted it if I made the alternative decision and not taken that ride. It was a catalyst for trying so many new things that I had been afraid of my whole life.

This may sound like a silly little story, but my fears and insecurities held me back in my career too. I used to be afraid to speak up at work. I didn't want to sound dumb. I didn't want to create waves or upset anyone. I showed up. I did my job. I did it well, but not too well. I was in the middle of the group. Average at best. I could have coasted through and done just fine. Luckily, I had the most amazing mentor come into my life at the perfect time. I was just coming out of my divorce and starting to semi-function again. I was at a pivotal point in my career. Again, I had to choose a path. I could take the advice I was being given even though I was afraid to go down an unfamiliar path, or I could live with my fear and keep on the same road that leads right to mediocrity. I chose option A. I chose to face my fears and take the advice of someone smarter and wiser than me. To listen to the voice of someone with experience and knowledge. Having a mentor who believed in me, encouraged me, and pushed me to the next level made me believe in myself. I pushed that fear to the side, said screw mediocrity and complacency, started voicing my opinions, and before I knew it, I went from the middle of the pack to number one. Turn to those people in your life that see the potential and greatness in you. Quit worrying about what the haters and doubters are saying. Those are the people that want you to fail. Turn the voice of THAT GUY off and listen to the voices of positivity and encouragement. The impact my mentor had on me has been significant and lasting. I let his voice replace the voices of those who said I couldn't do it. The ones who said I wasn't good enough. His advice, support, and encouragement made my confidence soar, and soon I became his "Superstar" and I am eternally grateful that he came into my life and that I didn't allow fear to hold me back from taking his advice. He pushed me out of my comfort zone and onto my path of greatness. (Thank you BJH).

It's okay to be afraid to be scared. It's not okay to let fear hold you back from all of the good things that are waiting for you out there. So do it. Say it out loud, "I'm scared as hell, but here goes nothing." What's the worst thing that could happen?

It's also okay to ask for help if you are scared. Our friends and family can be great support systems, but they are not medical professionals. They can give advice and try to help you through it, but it's not the same as seeking the care of a professional. It can be very difficult to admit we need help, but please do not be ashamed or embarrassed to seek treatment. I was spiraling out of control, trying my best to get through each day. I was surviving at best, but I wasn't thriving. Everything was difficult and even simple things seemed insurmountable. It wasn't that I didn't want to seek help, I just didn't know where to start. At the urging of my friends, I set up an appointment with a counselor and nurse practitioner to put together an action plan to help me get through and come out on the other side. The combination of medication and therapy was a game-changer. Even though I was fighting as hard as I could, I was so much better equipped to handle the sh*t that was being thrown at me once we figured out the best treatment plan. There's no shame in my game. I needed help and I'm not afraid to admit it. I am so glad that I did. Get the help you need. Use all the resources you have available. Don't for one second feel embarrassed or ashamed if you need counseling or medication or both. Getting the treatment you need can make all the difference in the world! Remember that list of resources we made a few pages back? Did you use any of them yet? Have you called and made any appointments? If the answer is no, then you better get to it now that we've pushed through the fear and self doubt.

PUSH YOUR BOUNDARIES OR YOU WILL BE LIMITED BY THEM.

Define or Redefine

You've got a choice to make. Are you going to let this experience define you and possibly destroy you, or are you going to learn from it and re-define yourself? You're at a crossroads. Which way are you going to choose to go? That little word "choose" is important. At this moment, you have a choice. What path will you take? The path to the top may not be the easiest or smoothest, but it does have the best view. You're not going to just open your eyes and be on top. You have to earn it, have to be prepared to do the work required to get there! Rehashing the details, feeling sorry for yourself, being bitter, won't get you anywhere. You will remain in that cycle until you choose to get out of it. Nobody said what happened was fair or that you deserved it, but if you don't pull yourself out of that negative space, you will go down a very dark path that leads to nowhere. Choose to take this awful experience and learn from it. Use this as an opportunity to reinvent yourself and decide what you want out of life. Are you willing to settle for less than you deserve? If you are, you might as well put this book down and concede to a life of mediocrity. If you don't want to push yourself to be the best you can be, then you might as well not spend the time or energy into reading any further. Do you love and value yourself enough to put in the work? You should, because you are worth it and you should never settle for less than what you deserve. It's time to erase that negative self talk that's holding you back and change the narrative.

It may seem like I'm over simplifying this, like undoing years of damage can just be erased in the blink of an eye. I'm not suggesting that at all. I get it. You're tired. Some days you barely get through, so how are you supposed to muster the energy it will take to get to the next level? I'm here to tell you that you will have to dig deep. You will have to tap into power reserves that are only used as emergency backups. You will have to find the will and the strength you never thought you would have. You can and you will. I CAN. I WILL. I MUST.

I just couldn't picture my life without my ex. How could he do this to me? How would I ever go on? I obsessed over those questions searching for the answers. I just couldn't envision my life any other way. We become accustomed to living a certain way whether it's good or bad, the idea of it being anything different than what you are used to is daunting. And here we are again, back to being paralyzed by the fear of change. Why do we hate it so much?

That's where I found myself. I had been unhappy for a long time, but I was used to it. It wasn't like one day we had a picture-perfect marriage and the next day my life was in shambles. It took many years of fighting, breaking up, and making up, mental and emotional abuse, and more tears than anyone should ever have to shed, and now that it was coming to an end I was fighting as hard as possible to keep it together. Why in the hell would I want to continue the rest of my life in that type of negative, abusive environment? Was I out of my mind?! What I had now was an opportunity to start over. To take my life in whatever direction I wanted. Instead of focusing on what was "taken" or what was changing, my mindset had to switch to "what can I take away from this experience? How can I make myself better?" I allowed the unhappy marriage to define me for way too long. I had let myself go down a dark path, and I had a lot of work to do if I wanted to get moving in the other direction. I knew I had to choose to do the work that had to be done if I wanted to get where I wanted and deserved to be. I couldn't let that guy define me or destroy me. I would fight back. I would claw my way out of the dark place and get over to the place of goodness and light. It was there waiting for me, I just had to find a way to get there from here, put one foot in front of the other, and get started! Take your pain and turn it into power. Redefine yourself. What do you want out of life? Don't just say it, you have to do it. Words minus action equal nothing (Words-Actions=Nothing). I started writing down my goals and making checklists, but more importantly, I did the necessary actionable items to achieve said goals. Instead of self-destructing, I was able to turn this into a chance for immeasurable personal growth. I was blessed with the chance to not only reflect on who I was, but who I wanted to be. F*ck that guy! It's time to flip the script and get to the top!

BA B*tch

Hi. My name is Shennoah and I'm a freaking badass b*tch. I have a successful career, an amazing family, and a budding business. I have overcome my fears, taken lessons away from my negative experiences, and chosen to grow from them. I have adapted when things didn't go according to plan and made the conscious decision to own and love who I am. Admittedly, I am far from perfect and I accept that. But I am striving to be better and do better every day. I am working on being more accepting and loving toward others and myself. I am also at a point where other people's opinions of me really don't matter. I guess you could say I'm out of f*cks to give. Ever since I ran out of f*cks to give about what others think of me, I have found myself much happier, more confident, and more self-assured than ever. The qualities that others identify in me as negative traits are the exact things I like about myself. It wasn't always that way though. I wasn't always able to like and accept all of the dimensions of my personality. People have told me for years that I'm intense, persistent, aggressive, and "a lot to handle." I've heard more than a few times that I look mean or unapproachable, that I'm intimidating. I never really could figure out why anyone would be intimidated by me. I wasn't purposefully trying to scare or intimidate people. It used to bother me so much that those were people's perceptions of me. The keyword is USED to bother me. I found that as soon as I started not giving a f*ck about what other people thought about me, the better my life got. If you want to live and enjoy your life to the fullest, you can't give a flying F*CK about what other people think about you. It's your life, not theirs. If you let other people's judgments influence your decisions you will never be happy. Why do you care what Becky down the road thinks about the car you drive or how you parent your kids or anything else? Do you want to put on a façade for other people or do you want to be authentically who YOU are and live your life the way you want to? Seems like a no-brainer to me, but like I said, I ran out of f*cks to give many years ago. Now I just do me. Whether you like me or hate me is up to you. It just doesn't make a difference to me. The key to being truly happy is being authentic and real. I used to worry so much about people not liking me that I tried to censor myself for certain people or certain situations, but as my self-evolution continued, I realized that the lack of authenticity only made me seem disingenuous and unrelatable to people. When I let the real me out, I found that some people liked me and some didn't and that's ok. If people are going to like me, I want them to like the real, raw, unfiltered, authentic me. Be unapologetically who you are and the right people will come into your life.

I am intense, aggressive, assertive, and a whole lot of EXTRA. But I'm equally kind, generous, loving, and loyal. I am passionate, driven, and motivated and that scares the bejesus out of some people. Too often people just want to blend in or go with the flow. They aim for the status quo so they don't get noticed or rock the boat. They get up, do what is expected of them and go to bed. No f*cking thank you. That is not the life for me. All the years I spent trying to make other people happy got me nowhere. I did what I thought I was supposed to do. I followed and conformed to the social "norms." I tried (unsuccessfully) to contain my extraness. I tried to be less direct and assertive so people wouldn't think I was mean, until I quit caring if people thought I was mean or not. I know I'm not mean. The people in my inner circle know that I love with a ferocity that is next level. I would do anything for those I care about. Being direct, knowing what I want, that is not mean. It's called confidence and self-assuredness. Being mean is when you intentionally try to do harm or hurt others. That statement does not reflect who I am at all. One day it dawned on me that all the words that people were using in a derogatory context to describe me were words that had a positive connotation to me. I love that I am passionate, intense, and persistent. Those qualities are some of the things that have helped me get where I am personally and professionally. My unwillingness to accept defeat pushed me through some of the most adverse times of my life. That inner fighter is what kept me going through the most painful and traumatizing events of my life. There were so many times I wanted to give up, but that voice inside me wouldn't let me give up or give in. If I didn't possess the inner strength that I have, I don't know where I would be today. The mental and emotional abuse would have destroyed a weaker individual. Don't get me wrong. It took its toll on me. I survived it because I am a survivor and that's what I had to do, but I'm not claiming I was the best version of myself. Some days I just pushed through. It was painful and exhausting and draining. I didn't know what to do, so I just stayed and put up with it. I let that guy drain my soul and my spirit day in and day out. I fought to keep my marriage and my family together because that's what you're supposed to do. That's what we're expected to do. To put up with sh*t we don't want to put up with or live a life that is less than we deserve. I didn't want to be a failure. I didn't want people to think I was a quitter or a bad person, mother, or wife. So, I stayed and I literally cried every single day. It was like a goddamn emotional roll-ercoaster. I felt like I was losing my mind.

You may know the feeling. You may be at a point when you think you don't have the energy to keep going. I was exhausted and tired of the fight, but that voice, that little voice in my head just kept saying, "Get the f*ck up. This fight's not over yet." You've got to get up. That badass b*tch, she is in there and she will help you get to the other side, but you have to let her out. You have to love and accept her the way she is. Let her insecurities become her source of strength and power. Write down the things you love about her and nurture those. Flip the script on the haters and use their negative words to create a positive script for yourself. If you turn the nega-tive into positive you take their power to hurt you away.

What words have others used to describe you in a negative light that you can turn into positive attributes? Write them down and associate a positive with each one. Turn your pain into power!!

Who are you? Who do you want to be??

What are your strengths?

What do you love about yourself?

_____

_____

_____

_____

_____

_____

_____

_____

_____

_____

_____

_____

_____

Check Yourself Before You Wreck Yourself

That was a great exercise in owning who you are and being a freaking badass, but don't get it twisted. I like who I am. I own the good and the bad, but that does not equate to me thinking I am perfect. Being confident does not give you the right to go around acting like a dick! I am happy with who I am, but I want to continually learn and grow as a person. I never want to become complacent or stagnant. Part of self-growth is the ability to be self-aware. Even though I acknowledge and like my assertive, confident attitude, it does not mean I don't realize there are some instances and situations that require a softer or less intense approach. I can own my power and strength, but at the same time not let that strength be unnecessarily overbearing or overwhelming to others around me. I am getting better at this, but it is still an area that I can use some improvement on. And guess what? That's ok. I recognize the areas that I need to be more self-aware about and I strive to improve every day. If I feel that I come across too strong or too aggressive toward someone or a particular situation, I have no qualms apologizing and trying a different approach. You have to be willing to identify the areas you can improve on if you want to get better at this thing called life. Being a confident chick is cool. Being an arrogant b*tch is not. I have the most amazing inner circle of strong, successful, badass b*tches that love and support each other. We don't talk behind each other's backs or cut each other down. We uplift and encourage one another. We listen to each other without judgment. We accept one another for who we are and we aren't afraid to call each other out. Those are real friends and that's how badass chicks do things. Wear your confidence like a badge of honor and use it to help others that may be struggling. Own your sh*t and be the best version of yourself. Trust me, it's a good look. Is there someone who helped you through a really tough time or situation? Someone who inspired you to try something new or get out of your comfort zone? Pay that sh*t forward! Help someone who is struggling. Motivate someone at work or in the gym. Share your story. You never know who it will help or inspire along the way.

Self-Awareness Check In

What do you want to work on?

How can you be the best version of yourself?

Are you paying it forward?

Are you surrounding yourself with the right people?

Before you can get where you want to go, you have to accept where you're at right now. Take a look around you. Is it good, bad, chaotic, crazy, messy, a freaking train wreck? It doesn't matter, because however your life is right now is your starting point. You've got to acknowledge how you got where you are and assess your state of affairs before you can decide where you want to go and how the f*ck you're going to get there. One of the biggest reasons people can't turn their lives around is that they refuse to believe they could do anything differently to change their circumstances. Instead of being proactive about assessing and addressing their issues, they just complain and keep doing what they're doing. I'm going to drop a real bombshell on you: If you want things to change, you're going to have to do something about it!!! Spoiler alert: Change requires action. You can keep b*tching and complaining and see where that gets you or you can change your mindset and take action. You need a new mentality. One of my favorite sayings "F*CK IT OR FIX IT." I admit that is a little aggressive, but let me explain. If there is something in your life that isn't working or someone who is bringing you down, you have the power to make a choice. If you believe there is nothing that you can do to change the outcome of the situation, it's time to stop wasting your energy and say "F*CK IT." Conversely, if you believe that if you put the time in and do the work, the situation or relationship will improve, then you can choose to "FIX IT."

This is not meant to trivialize what you are going through, but if you break something you have two options: 1. Throw it away and get a new one, or 2. spend the time/money to get it repaired. The same is true with our relationships, friendships, careers, bodies, and finances. You need to evaluate each area of your life and determine what needs to be done to have the most positive impact. What is working and what is not working for you? Let's make a F*CK IT COLUMN and a FIX IT COLUMN:

F*ck It

_____

_____

_____

_____

_____

_____

_____

_____

_____

_____

_____

_____

_____

_____

_____

_____

_____

_____

_____

_____

Fix It

_____

_____

_____

_____

_____

_____

_____

_____

_____

_____

_____

_____

_____

_____

_____

_____

_____

_____

_____

_____

Now that you've got your F*ck It or Fix It list, you have to figure out what actions to take to fix the things that are broken but you feel are worth repairing and you have to decide how to remove the things in the F*ck It column if they are not adding any value to your life. You have to start somewhere, so pick one thing from your list and take action. Then move on to the next one, then the next, until you've crossed everything off the list.

What wasn't working for me was being complacent. Thinking that I had to do things in a certain way or certain order. That didn't work for me. Trying to fit into the "box" or blend in was keeping me from reaching my full potential. I'm unique, so how am I supposed to think, act, dress, talk, and be like everyone else? And why would I want to? I like who I am, remember?

Those things that aren't just not working for you, but they're holding you back, say f*cking goodbye to them. Are you in a relationship where you can't be yourself? Get out of it. Is your job crushing your soul or turning your brain into mush? Time for a new one. Are you spinning your wheels at the gym and not getting results? Find a new plan. My point is STOP doing things that aren't working for you. Sure, you can't change jobs as easily as you can change gyms, but you can change any area of your life if you are willing to do the work. You know what Brittany says, "You better work b*tch."

Don't Change, Grow

People get so hung up on refusing to change that they miss growth opportunities. You don't have to change the core of your being to grow and become a better version of yourself. I believe we should always be evolving and looking for ways to improve ourselves. If you possess the ability to self-reflect and own your sh*t, good and bad, you open yourself up to a world of possibilities that aren't possible if you have an "I refuse to change" mindset. Growth and change are not necessarily synonymous. You don't have to change who you are to grow and evolve into who you want to be. Growth is not about being someone or something you're not. It's about being the best, most authentic version of the real you. That can take a lot of time and a lot of trial and error. There are going to be bumps along your path to greatness. You're gonna make mistakes. You're gonna f*ck up. The important part is to take a lesson away from those screw-ups. Don't keep making the same mistakes. That's not growth, it's stupidity. Take the time to evaluate and assess the situation. Could you have done something differently to change the outcome? Okay. So, keep it moving and try a different approach next time. You're still you. You didn't change, you learned and grew. Now ain't that some deep sh*t.

I dated a guy who was so adamant that he wasn't going to change for anyone that he couldn't enjoy anything if it wasn't what he wanted to do. Before I started dating him, I had heard (through my detective work) that he was "a nice guy, but he didn't compromise." Over and over that is what everyone said. After the hell I had been through, a "nice guy" sounded like a welcome change. I didn't fully grasp what they meant when they said "he refused to change or he refused to compromise." I didn't want to change anyone. I wanted someone who knew who they were and would appreciate who I was. Two independent, self-sufficient people who compliment one another is what I wanted. I didn't want to mold someone into what I wanted and I didn't want that done for me. I was, however, willing to learn and grow in a relationship. I was ready to have someone who brought out the best in me and made me want to be the best version of myself possible. Now don't get it twisted, I am 100% against changing who you are to make someone else happy. You should never compromise your core values to fit someone else's narrative. I'm not suggesting you sacrifice your values, beliefs, politics, etc. to make another person happy. I think it is important that those points align, or are at least complimentary with the person you choose to be your life partner. What I'm talking about is being open and receptive to new experiences and opportunities. Not being so stubborn or "set in your ways" that you won't try new things. It is important to find ways to connect with your partner. I felt like so many opportunities to bond and connect with my boyfriend were missed because if we weren't doing what he wanted, he never seemed to enjoy himself. After enough nagging, he would sometimes try the things I enjoyed, but it felt like pulling teeth, and created a less than enjoyable experience. His interest in me and the things I cared about and enjoyed were disingenuous at best. He wasn't going to change for me and that was that. Growth, adventure, and experiences were missed all in the name of not changing. Had he been open to trying new things he may have learned more about me and discovered new things he enjoyed along the way. When you take an interest and participate in the things your partner is passionate about it also shows that you care and that the things they love are important to you, and the same goes vice versa. Whether you like it or hate it, you will be creating memories together and strengthening your connection with that person. That's what relationships are about: growing, connecting, learning together.

As you move forward in this process and on your journey, don't let anyone inhibit your ability to achieve everything you want in every area of your life. Complacency is among my biggest pet peeves. Do you want to be stagnant and complacent or do you want to accomplish new things and crush your goals? Life is about exploration and experiences. Don't let it pass you by. Open yourself up and let life in. Sometimes that is scary. It means being vulnerable and exposed. It means looking your fears in the eye and saying "you're not going to hold me back."

So don't change my friend — GROW!

PUSH YOUR BOUNDARIES OR YOU WILL BE LIMITED BY THEM.

No Looking Back

Now that you've made it all this way, do me a favor. Don't you dare look in the rear-view mirror. Don't let the "what ifs" creep into your head and create doubt. Don't question yourself or your decisions. Don't waste time thinking about what you could have done differently. Don't play out different hypothetical scenarios. And most importantly, don't worry about where your ex is or what he's doing. That's not your concern. You are on a new journey and a new path now. There is nothing behind you to see. You need to focus on what lies ahead. Think about all you have been through. You have overcome and survived so much. You've shed many tears and now it's time to wipe them away and replace the crying with laughter. Replace the pain with power. Trade in the sadness for joy. Be done with the negativity and gloom and doom. It is your time to shine. This is going to be so amazing. You are going to shock yourself with the direction your life goes. You won't wish you had him back, but you will wonder why you didn't do this sooner. Your strength and resiliency will give you the confidence to conquer any challenges life throws your way. You can do this. You know how I know? Because I did it. I thought my divorce was the worst thing that could ever happen to me. The pain, the heart-break, the embarrassment. There couldn't possibly be anything worse. I would never love again. I would never recover financially. I couldn't go on if I didn't have him. Yeah, all of that turned out to be completely false. What I thought was the worst thing that could happen to me turned out to be the exact opposite. It was the best freaking thing that could have ever happened to me. You may not realize that now, but one day your lightbulb will go off too and you'll realize you're right where you need to be.

Time of My Life

Okay. Here we are. The final chapter of this book and the first chapter of your new life. Are you ready to rewrite your story? Did you do the hard work? Are you ready to start living your best life? I hope by the time you get to this chapter you are feeling more powerful and more confident. I hope your mindset has changed and your pain is turning into power. I hope you feel alive, motivated, and inspired. I hope you are ready to receive all the blessings and goodness that the universe has in store for you. You are worth it and you deserve all the good things that come your way. Let the good vibes flow into your life and don't you dare look in that rear view mirror. It is time to move forward. Don't let life pass you by. Take advantage of every opportunity that comes your way. Never miss an opportunity for a new adventure or experience. If something scares you, do it anyway. Try new things. If you don't put yourself out there you may miss the opportunity of a lifetime. Celebrate yourself and how far you've come.

I never expected I would feel so different when my divorce was finalized, but I did. It was like I could feel the weight of all the negativity and stress be lifted off of me. It felt like it had been raining for months and then suddenly, it stopped, the clouds parted, and a rainbow appeared. Okay, that's a bit melodramatic, but it honestly felt like a re-birth. The world didn't stop, but I was ready to rejoin the land of the living. I had survived the storm I was convinced would destroy me and make it impossible to rebuild, but there I stood. I was not unscathed, but I was intact enough to start over. I could rebuild myself and my life however I wanted, and so I did. Once I stopped being afraid, the possibilities were endless to me. My life became happier and more exciting. My mind was clearer and my creativity skyrocketed. You will be amazed at all the things you are capable of now that you have cleared your mind and your life of all the negative people and forces. I have a feeling you are going to surprise yourself as I did at all of the things you can accomplish. When I reclaimed my power, my career took off, my relationships flourished, I traveled more than ever, I celebrated the big and small triumphs, and began really enjoying my life. I was so afraid to go on without him and wouldn't you know it HE was the one holding me back. This whole time he was standing in the way of my greatness. Who knows how many opportunities and experiences I missed out on, but you know what, I can't focus on that. I told you not to look in the rearview mirror and I'm a proponent of practicing what I preach. So, f*ck that guy, and f*ck whoever hurt you.

This is your new beginning. Your chance to explore and see the world in a whole new light as a whole new you. There are places to go and people to see. What have you wanted to do or try that you never had the opportunity or courage to do? Do it now! Make yourself a list of the things that are most important to you and start checking them off. I mean it! Literally, make a list and start doing it. You got this b*tch! Let that light shine!

I am going to try

_____

_____

_____

I am going to book a trip to

_____

_____

_____

I am going to start a new

_____

_____

_____

I am going to set a goal to

_____

_____

_____

_____

_____

_____

_____

_____

_____

DON'T LOSE YOUR SH*T CHECKLIST

☐ **FIND YOUR ZEN**

No doubt this is a stressful and emotional time. It is critical that you find time to quiet your mind and center yourself before you lose it. Try a mindful practice like yoga, meditation or prayer. #Dontloseyourshi*t

☐ **RELAX AND UNWIND**

I'm sure it feels like you're carrying the weight of the world on your shoulders. Take some time to chillax. Schedule a massage or a manicure, get your hair did, or pour a glass of wine and soak your woes in a bubble bath before that weight crushes you. #Dontloseyoursh*t

☐ **PHONE A FRIEND**

Nobody said you have to go through this alone, so don't. Pick up the phone and call a friend for advice, emotional support, or just some good chit chat to change your mood. Them b*tches love ya so call them when you need them. #Dontloseyoursh*t

WORK YO' BODY

Stress can manifest itself into physical symptoms so it's important to keep that body strong and healthy. Go for a run, take a class at the gym, jump on your spin bike or take a walk to blow off some steam and get the feel good endorphins flowing. #Dontloseyoursh*t

TRY SOMETHING NEW

Negative energy and vibes will drag you down and make it impossible to pull yourself out of this funk. Re-direct all that negative juju in a positive direction. Give a new hobby a try, sign up for a class or workshop, go somewhere you've never been. Whatever it is that you've been putting off or afraid to try, DO IT NOW and turn a negative into a positive. #Dontloseyoursh*t

TAKE A CHILL PILL

The chaos you are dealing with will reek havoc on your mental and physical health if you don't get the treatment you need. I can't emphasize enough that there is no shame in asking for professional help. Make an appointment with a doctor, therapist, counselor, or all of the above to get the treatment plan you need. #Dontloseyoursh*t

TAKE A BREAK

You have to know when to step away from everything and give yourself time to hit reset. You will be better equipped to deal with difficult situations if you take the time to step away and regroup. Attend a retreat, spa day, or a weekend getaway to give yourself a break from all the drama for a hot second. #Don'tloseyoursh*t

BREATH

You feel your blood pressure rise and your heart rate accelerate- STOP! Close your eyes, take a deep breath and count to 10, or 20 or 100. Count as high as you need to until you calm down. In through the nose, out through the mouth until you feel that blood pressure come back to normal. #Dontloseyoursh*t

 SCREAM & SHOUT (AND LET IT ALL OUT)

Ok. So you've taken all the deep breaths you can take and counted higher than you thought you knew how, but it's not working. Time for a different tactic: Unleash it! Scream, yell, cry do whatever you need to do to let those pent up feelings out. Just do it in a safe space and environment. Scream at the top of your lungs in your car or into pillow or have a good cry in the shower and let it wash your tears down the drain. It can be cathardic to allow yourself to feel your feelings and let them out just don't unleash the beast in the wrong place or on the wrong person. #Dontloseyoursh*t

PAUSE FOR THE CAUSE

I know it is easy to act on emotion or impulse, but that can cause you more issues and headaches to deal with. So before you make that knee jerk reaction, pause and think about the possible consequences. Rember this acronym: NLN (Now. Later. Never). Ask yourself, is there benefit in saying this now, later, or never? Don't let emotions overpower intelligence. #Dontloseyoursh*t

F*CK THAT GUY: BADASS B*TCH 2.0 CHECKLIST

☐ DO YOU BOO BOO

No doubt you haven't been living up to your full potential. It's time to make yourself a priority and being the baddest, badass b*tch you can be. Let her out! She's free to be who she wants to be now. #F*ckthatguy

What are your top 3 priorities?:

1. _____

_____

_____

2. _____

_____

_____

3. _____

_____

_____

TURN THE WORST THING THAT HAPPENED TO YOU INTO THE BEST THING

We can learn and grow from any situation especially the most difficult ones. Time to find the silver lining and find some positive takeaways. You have the power to change your mindset and your circumstances. #F*ckthatguy

Below identify the mistakes you made and how you can learn from them. How can you take a negative experience and grow from it? What are the biggest lessons you learned? What can you do to not make the same mistakes again?

☐ LEVEL UP

Time to take your game to the next level. You've got your priorities in check and you're turning negatives into positives. Time to take your game to the next level and become the best version of you! Mediocrity and complacency don't live here! #F*ckthatguy

Strengths   ## Room For Improvement

—————————————   —————————————

—————————————   —————————————

—————————————   —————————————

—————————————   —————————————

—————————————   —————————————

—————————————   —————————————

—————————————   —————————————

—————————————   —————————————

—————————————   —————————————

—————————————   —————————————

—————————————   —————————————

—————————————   —————————————

—————————————   —————————————

—————————————   —————————————

NO TURNING BACK

There's no time for second guessing yourself. It's full steam ahead for this girl. There's nothing in the rearview mirror worth turning around for. It's time to decide where this new road will take you and keep your eyes on the journey waiting for you. New places and new beginnings girl! #F*ckthatguy

What direction are you going to take your life in? Where does your journey begin? What do you want to see along the way?

_____

_____

_____

_____

_____

_____

_____

_____

_____

_____

_____

_____

_____

_____

_____

_____

TURN THE BEAT AROUND

Now that your life is headed in a new direction it's time to find a new beat to dance to. No more sad songs to sing around here girl. Set your soul on fire, find a new rhythm, and drop some new beats! #F*ckthatguy

List your favorite feel good tunes and create your new you playlist!

1.

2.

3.

4.

5.

6.

7.

8.

9.

10.

GET OUT OF YOUR COMFORT ZONE

If you really want to challenge yourself to make changes it's time you step out of your comfort zone and try things that you never thought you would. Maybe you were to scared to try them or someone told you that you wouldn't be able to. Well it's time to do it now b*tch! Shock everyone, especially yourself with your new fearless attitude. #F*ckthatguy

Time for an action plan. What is something you've always wanted to try? What has fear held you back from doing? What couldn't you do before that you have the strength and confidence to do now? Don't just write them down. Push through the fear and anxiety and go and do it!

Yo B*tch! You've got the tools now it's time to get it gear and start making sh*t happen. Keep your checklists handy so you can remind yourself where you're going and what you're made of!

TURN YOUR PAIN INTO POWER ACTION PLAN

WORDS-ACTIONS=NOTHING

Acknowledgements

To the most selfless woman I know, my mom, I cannot express the gratitude and admiration I have for you. I am here because of you. I made it through because of your unconditional love. Thank you for lending me your strength when I had none. Thank you for loving me when I wasn't deserving of it. This life and this journey I owe to you.

To Jeremiah, thank you for constantly reminding me to trust God's plan for me because he is in control.

A special shout out to my soul sister Stephanie for not only her loyalty and support, but for making the title of this book possible.

Thank you Amy for being my ride or die and always having bail money and a first aid kit ready and waiting.

And to my framily, my brothers, my mentor (BJH), and my entire tribe, thank you for showing up and showing out when I needed you the most. Thank you for being there on my darkest days and making sure I got back up to fight. Thank you for your love, support, honesty, loyalty, and friendship.

Mike (BMBF), I'm so glad this crazy life led me to a new beginning with you. The best is yet to come. ♥

CPSIA information can be obtained
at www.ICGtesting.com
Printed in the USA
LVHW091626090222
710692LV00002B/110